CHALLENGE

A GUIDE TO PREPARE STUDENT LEADERS
FOR SPIRIT-EMPOWERED CAMPUS MINISTRY

NATALIE AND JOE BARNOSKE

Edited by Jared Stump
Design by Joe Barnoske

Published in Dallas, Texas, by Battle Ground Creative
In Association with Youth Alive Pen Florida
First Edition

Battle Ground Creative is a faith-based publishing company with an emphasis on helping first–time authors find their voice. Named after an obscure city in Washington State, we currently operate offices in Dallas, Texas and Harrisburg, Pennsylvania. For a complete title list and bulk order information, please visit www.battlegroundcreative.com

ISBN-10: 099087382X
ISBN-13: 978-0-9908738-2-2
RELIGION / Devotional / Youth Ministry

Printed in the United States of America

*This challenge is dedicated to Pastor Johnnie Wilson.
Thank you for pouring so many years into youth ministry.
You will always be our youth pastor.*

TABLE OF CONTENTS

WELCOME TO THE
EmpowerME Challenge

THIS IS A CALL TO ACTION

A challenge that will stretch
you beyond your limits.

Are you ready to take the EmpowerME Challenge?

For 5 weeks, will you commit to give everything you have to go where you've never been? This is not just a devotional. It is a challenge that must start and end with you. It is a guide to empowerment, but you must take the journey with the Holy Spirit yourself.

CALLING ALL CAMPUS MISSIONARIES!

Did you know that one of the greatest mission fields is your school?

A mission field calls for a missionary.
Student, you are that missionary!

Campus Missionaries, it is time to arise
out of the pain, fear, and lies of the enemy into the power that God has for your future.

A CAMPUS MISSIONARY
commits to be a leader on God's mission at their school.

THERE IS A MISSION AT HAND:
to reach the lost and hurting at your campus.

BUT GOD DOES NOT SEND YOU OUT ALONE.
He has given you a helper.

THE HOLY SPIRIT.
Your guide. Your comforter. Your friend.

Do you know the Holy Spirit?

P2

UNCOMMON OUTPOURING

For ten days, 120 of the disciples waited, prayed, and fasted for something uncommon to happen in their generation.

On the day of Pentecost, they were gathered together when the sound of a strong wind filled the house. When they looked up, it appeared as though tongues of fire spread out and touched each person. The next thing they knew, each one began to speak in other languages.

Of course, when the Spirit moves there are always mockers! Some made fun of the disciples, saying that they were drunk. Peter, usually the first to hide from ridicule, stood up with new power and began to preach with boldness. He saw 3,000 people come to Christ because the Holy Spirit had been poured out.

From that day on, everywhere the disciples went they prayed for people to receive the Holy Spirit... and they did! (Acts 8:14-17, 9:17, 19:2,6)

FAST FORWARD 2000+ YEARS

Today, the Holy Spirit is still empowering people to witness. The world has not improved, so how much more do we need the Holy Spirit today?

When you surrender your life to the Lord, the Holy Spirit comes inside your heart. If you need to surrender your life to God, pray right now that He would forgive you, and ask Him to enter your heart. You can go to the resources tab of the PF Youth Alive mobile app to find out more information.

We believe that God wants to give you a greater outpouring of the Holy Spirit so that you can be a light in one of the darkest places of the world: YOUR SCHOOL.

Just like the disciples, God wants you to be on an exciting journey of learning how to work with the Holy Spirit to reach the people around you!

Let's start by looking at how this guide works.

INTRODUCTION
How this works...

The daily chart is one of the most important parts of this journey. It is a tool to help you make your time with God a priority. At the end of each day, there is a blank to write down your appointment with God for the next day. This is not about merely punching a time clock, but keeping your promise to God.

"Where and when you have your time with God is of utmost importance. The more seriously that you take these times, the more beneficial they will be to you."

Pastor Johnnie Wilson
Lead Youth Pastor
Mainstream Orlando

☑ **Daily Bible Reading:** You will see one chapter listed to read each day. Don't rush it, listen to what the Holy Spirit is saying!

☑ **Daily Prayer and Worship Times:** Set aside time every day to build an intimate relationship with God. Pray daily for the things on your prayer list. Also, make time to worship God—maybe start with one song before school in the morning and increase!

Lines are provided so you can write down what God spoke to you through these prayer and worship times.

☑ **Daily Power Challenge:** At the end of each lesson you will be challenged to take an action step at your campus! These important challenges will put your faith into practice.

The best way to do the weekly lesson is with a group, but the daily challenges are your responsibility. Get accountability—it is a challenge for a reason!

Weekly Group Lesson: Stay accountable during the challenge.
Testimony Challenge: Learn how to share your testimony.
Witness Challenge: Share your faith with at least one person.
Spiritual Gifts Challenge: Learn more about the gifts that God has given you to reach your world! Download at pfyouthalive.com or on the mobile app.

W1 PRAY
TUESDAY

DATE: 7/14/15

☒ Read: Acts 2 ☒ 30min Personal Prayer ☒ 15min Worship
☒ DAILY CHALLENGE:

Put together a prayer list for this journey - Use the
prayer list at the end of each lesson to help you.
Pray through this list starting today!

What did God say to you in personal prayer time?
(If nothing, that's ok! Just grow in your listening.)

_God has challenged me to be more
of an example to those around me._

What scripture stood out to you from the daily reading?

_2:11 - "They're speaking our languages,
describing God's mighty works!"_

What did this scripture reveal to you? _The Holy Spirit
filled the disciples so that others
would come to accept forgiveness._

How does this understanding apply to your life? _God can
use anyone in any place to share His
message of hope. He wants to use me_

We encourage you to write down a prayer that God would help
you live out this understanding. _God Help me to be
like the early church. I want to be
bold in my walk with you. Never ashamed_

My appointment with
God tomorrow is at   2 : 30 pm

TAKE ON THE CHALLENGE

THE LIE
- The Holy Spirit is not as important as God and Jesus
- The Holy Spirit is someTHING that can help you be a better Christian
- The Holy Spirit only helped people in ancient days

THE TRUTH
- The Holy Spirit is an equal member of the Trinity and empowers us! (1 John 5:6-8)
- The Holy Spirit is someONE who wants a relationship with you and feels sad when ignored. (John 14:16-17, 23; Eph. 4:30)
- The Holy Spirit is still speaking to and filling people today! (Joel 2:28)

The Holy Spirit wants to empower you; this means He wants to FILL you with POWER so that you can grow closer to God and make a difference in the world around you.

"You will receive POWER when the Holy Spirit comes on you, And you will be my witnesses, telling people about me everywhere..." Acts 1:8 (NLT)

Are you ready to grow closer to God than you ever have before? Are you ready to become the campus missionary that God has called you to be?

START BY PRAYING
THIS PRAYER OUT LOUD AND FROM YOUR HEART:

Dear Jesus,

Thank You for sending the Holy Spirit to be my comforter and friend. Holy Spirit, I recognize that You are an equal member of the Trinity and that You want to empower me. So, I ask you, to fill me with all of You so that I can grow closer to God and be a witness. Let your power overflow from my heart so that others know I am a disciple of Jesus. I pray for miracles, prophecy, tongues, and whatever other gifts You desire in my life so that I can see revival. Help me to put 100% into the EmpowerME challenge, so that I can get everything from it that You have for me.

In the name of Jesus Christ, Amen.

Your journey with the Holy Spirit begins NOW!

W1 EMPOWERED TO PRAY

The Numbers:
- 76% of Americans believe that a constitutional amendment to allow voluntary prayer in public schools is a good thing.
- 23% oppose bringing prayer back into public schools.
- Only 3.3% say that they pray for strangers.
- 49% of teens say they would attend a prayer meeting before or after school if asked.[1]

So, why don't we pray more?

Here are the most common excuses:
- "Prayer is boring."
- "I can't hear God when I pray."
- "I'm too busy to pray."

What is your biggest excuse?

_____

We know that we need to pray more, but why does it often feel like our prayers are dead and dry?

▶▶ It's because we are missing the power of the Holy Spirit in our prayers! ◀◀

If prayer is the ultimate cell phone, then the Holy Spirit is the invisible sound wave that connects our prayers to God. You can't see it, but it's there! When we are tuned in to the Spirit, we don't hear static; instead, we can hear God's voice clearly.

"And the Holy Spirit helps us in our weakness. For example, we don't know what God wants us to pray for. But the Holy Spirit prays for us with groanings that cannot be expressed in words." Romans 8:26 (NLT)

Do you need help praying? Ask the Holy Spirit for help.

P8

The Holy Spirit helps us...

PRAY WITH POSITION

There is something special that happens when we pause our day and get alone with God. This positions us to pray with no distractions. What is best for you: In nature, a prayer walk, a prayer chair, or a quiet corner? Whatever it may be, set aside time each day for just you and God.

Also, position yourself spiritually by praying with confidence! The Holy Spirit gives you boldness to pray prayers that please God.

PRAY WITH PURPOSE

Here is a simple format that can help you begin to pray:

- **Pray Upward:** Give God praise for all He has done.
- **Pray Downward:** Pray against the enemy's plans.
- **Pray Inward:** Pray for yourself. (struggles, questions, decisions)
- **Pray Outward:** Pray for others.
- **Pray Forward:** Pray with expectation for the future.
- **Pray Backward:** Thank God for the blessings in your life.

Invite the Holy Spirit into your prayer times, and He will show you the position, purpose, and power of prayer uniquely meant for you!

PRAY WITH POWER (JOSHUA CH.6)

The Israelites circled the city of Jericho one time for six days, and then seven times on the seventh day. Imagine how strange they looked marching circles around an entire city! But from their obedience and consistency in prayer, God brought the walls of Jericho crashing down with a powerful shout of victory.

Guess what? YOUR SCHOOL is YOUR JERICHO! It is time for spiritual warfare at your campus. Start circling your school in prayer and watch God bring walls crashing to the ground!

P9

WHAT DOES THIS MEAN FOR MY CAMPUS?

Tim Tebow understands the importance of prayer:

"It's OK to be outspoken about your faith ..." [2]
"I pray to start my day, and finish it in prayer." [3]

Setting aside time to pray every day will help you walk in boldness! Imagine walking down the hallways of your school or home praying in the power of the Holy Spirit. If a generation began walking in the power of prayer, anything would be possible!

THINK ABOUT IT...

How will prayer help your campus? Think about praying for specific things, such as suicide or bullying.

_____

_____

How will you personally commit to pray for your campus this year?

_____

_____

This is my strategy to incorporate more prayer at my school:
(ex: in my club, prayer group, or prayer walks).

_____

_____

_____

WE ENCOURAGE YOU TO TALK TO YOUR
YOUTH PASTOR ABOUT DOING THIS STRATEGY!

WRITE YOUR PERSONAL TESTIMONY HERE

What was your life like before you knew Jesus? _____

_____

_____

_____

_____

_____

What led you to completely surrender your life to Jesus and how did it happen? _____

_____

_____

_____

_____

How is your life different now that you are living for Christ?

_____

_____

_____

_____

_____

_____

W1 PRAY
MONDAY

DATE:_____

☐ Read: Acts 1 ☐ 30min Personal Prayer ☐ 15min Worship
☐ DAILY CHALLENGE:

Download the Pen Florida Youth Alive App on your phone.
This is a great resource for reaching your campus!

What did God say to you in personal prayer time?
(If nothing, that's ok! Just grow in your listening.)

_____

_____

What scripture stood out to you from the daily reading?

_____

_____

What did this scripture reveal to you? _____

_____

_____

How does this understanding apply to your life? _____

_____

_____

We encourage you to write down a prayer that God would help
you live out this understanding. _____

_____

_____

My appointment with
God tomorrow is at   _____ : _____

W1 PRAY

TUESDAY

☐ Read: Acts 2 ☐ 30min Personal Prayer ☐ 15min Worship
☐ DAILY CHALLENGE:

Put together a prayer list for this journey - Use the
prayer list at the end of each lesson to help you.
Pray through this list starting today!

What did God say to you in personal prayer time?

_____

_____

What scripture stood out to you from the daily reading?

_____

_____

What did this scripture reveal to you? _____

_____

_____

How does this understanding apply to your life? _____

_____

_____

We encourage you to write down a prayer that God would help
you live out this understanding. _____

_____

_____

My appointment with
God tomorrow is at _____ : _____

P13

W1 PRAY
WEDNESDAY

DATE:_____

☐ Read: Acts 3 ☐ 30min Personal Prayer ☐ 15min Worship
☐ DAILY CHALLENGE:

What is keeping you from hearing God's voice: Do you need to forgive, let go, or surrender disbelief? Get right with God TODAY!

What did God say to you in personal prayer time?

_____

_____

What scripture stood out to you from the daily reading?

_____

_____

What did this scripture reveal to you? _____

_____

_____

How does this understanding apply to your life? _____

_____

_____

We encourage you to write down a prayer that God would help you live out this understanding. _____

_____

_____

P14

My appointment with God tomorrow is at _____:_____

W1 PRAY
THURSDAY

DATE:_____

☐ Read: Acts 4 ☐ 30min Personal Prayer ☐ 15min Worship
☐ DAILY CHALLENGE:

Memorize Romans 8:26-27. Do you want the Holy Spirit to pray through you? Talk with Him about it.

What did God say to you in personal prayer time?
_____
_____

What scripture stood out to you from the daily reading?
_____
_____

What did this scripture reveal to you? _____
_____
_____

How does this understanding apply to your life? _____
_____
_____

We encourage you to write down a prayer that God would help you live out this understanding. _____
_____
_____

My appointment with God tomorrow is at _____ : _____

P15

W1 PRAY

FRIDAY

DATE:_____

☐ Read: Acts 5 ☐ 30min Personal Prayer ☐ 15min Worship
☐ DAILY CHALLENGE:

Today, pray different than usual. Sit quietly in God's presence, go on a walk, or pray with someone. Prayer doesn't have to be the same.... Keep it fresh and exciting!

What did God say to you in personal prayer time?

_____

_____

What scripture stood out to you from the daily reading?

_____

_____

What did this scripture reveal to you? _____

_____

_____

How does this understanding apply to your life? _____

_____

_____

We encourage you to write down a prayer that God would help you live out this understanding. _____

_____

_____

My appointment with
God tomorrow is at _____ : _____

W1 PRAY

SATURDAY

DATE:_____

☐ Read: Acts 6 ☐ 30min Personal Prayer ☐ 15min Worship
☐ DAILY CHALLENGE:

Plan a prayer walk around your school with some friends just like when Joshua circled Jericho. Pray with the passion of Joshua, because your school is your Jericho!

What did God say to you in personal prayer time?

_____

_____

What scripture stood out to you from the daily reading?

_____

_____

What did this scripture reveal to you? _____

_____

_____

How does this understanding apply to your life? _____

_____

_____

We encourage you to write down a prayer that God would help you live out this understanding. _____

_____

_____

W1 PRAY
SUNDAY
DATE:_____

☐ Read: Acts 7 ☐ 30min Personal Prayer ☐ 15min Worship
☐ DAILY CHALLENGE:

If you haven't already, take time to write out your testimony in
the space provided on Page 11 of this book. Writing it
down will make it easier to share!

What did God say to you in personal prayer time?

_____

_____

What scripture stood out to you from the daily reading?

_____

_____

What did this scripture reveal to you? _____

_____

_____

How does this understanding apply to your life? _____

_____

_____

We encourage you to write down a prayer that God would help
you live out this understanding. _____

_____

_____

My appointment with
God tomorrow is at   _____ : _____

W1 PRAY

NOTES:

_____

_____

_____

_____

_____

_____

_____

PRAYER LIST:

Revival	Your Church	Your School
Family	Your Pastors	Your Principal
Friends	Missions	Your Teachers
The Lost	Personal Growth	Administration

_____

_____

_____

_____

_____

_____

W2 EMPOWERED TO OVERFLOW

Look at what Jesus said before He left the earth:

"If you love me, show it by doing what I've told you. I will talk to the Father, and he'll provide you another Friend so that you will always have someone with you. This Friend is the Spirit of Truth." John 14:15-17 (MSG)

What an extraordinary promise! There is Friend whom the Father will send, known as the Counselor, the Comforter, and the Spirit of Truth. This Friend will dwell inside our hearts, filling us with the goodness of God.... He is the Holy Spirit!

BUT please understand that the Holy Spirit does not fill us so that we can simply be full. He fills us so that we can OVERFLOW.

You are FILLED to OVERFLOW!

What does this mean? Probably not what you think! It does not just mean that we will walk in power and anointing. Although this will happen, it also means that we will overflow with the Fruit of the Spirit: *love, joy, peace, patience, goodness, kindness, faithfulness, gentleness, and self-control. (Galatians. 5:22)*

To overflow with the Fruit of the Spirit is what it truly means to be a disciple of Jesus Christ. If you preach the Word, but have no love, then it profits nothing. If you go on a mission trip or do ministry, but have no self-control, then there is a problem! God wants us to bear fruit that will last longer than any of our works.

"You did not choose me, but I chose you and appointed you so that you might go and BEAR FRUIT—FRUIT THAT WILL LAST..." John 15:16

The Fruit of the Spirit reveals the character of God in our hearts. God wants us to be filled with power, but just as importantly, He wants us to overflow with His character.

P20

Rate yourself on a scale from 1-10 in the following areas, with 10 being excellent and 1 being poor:

____ I can easily show love, regardless of who someone is or what they look like

____ I can easily stay joyful during difficult times

____ I can easily keep a mind of peace when I am overwhelmed or have a ton of responsibility

____ I can easily stay patient when others annoy me

____ I can choose goodness when its easier to disobey

____ I can choose kindness when its easier to be mean, prideful, or selfish

____ I can push myself to stay faithful, even when its easier to quit

____ I can easily keep my words gentle, even in the midst of a heated discussion

____ I choose self-control, even when I want to fall back into bad thoughts or actions

BASED ON THIS ANALYSIS, WHAT AREAS DO YOU STRUGGLE WITH THE MOST?

_____

How can you grow in the areas you struggle with?

_____

Remember, do not seek perfection; Seek progress! Cut off bad fruit by choosing to purposefully do the opposite of what you feel.

For example: You do not like someone at school, but every time you are tempted to talk bad about them you purposefully stop and pray for them instead. This shows that you choose **love, patience, and kindness over gossip.**

WHAT DOES THIS MEAN FOR MY CAMPUS?

"I didn't want to be like everyone else. I wanted to be better. If I did what everybody else did, then why would you look up to me?" [1]

Tim Tebow

With the help of the Holy Spirit, we can be better!

When we go through hard times, we can find joy in knowing that God is developing His character within us so that we can be an example to everyone around us.

What are you facing right now that you know God is using to develop the fruit in your life? You are NOT alone. Talk to a leader for help!

Also, take this advice from a student who went through a hard season with her campus club, but chose to never give up:

*"Put God first in everything! Stay passionate and loving, even if it seems unnoticed, because God has a plan. Stay committed and stay in prayer. **You may be the only BIBLE your campus will ever see.**"*

Taylor - Lakeland, FL

As a campus missionary, you will go through seasons where your club struggles or you feel rejected, but you must not quit! You will develop strong fruit and godly results if you choose to never give up.

Measure your success by God, not the opinion of others!

P22

THINK ABOUT IT...

What success have you had with campus ministry at your school, no matter how small or big?

_____

_____

_____

What was the most difficult moment you have experienced with doing campus ministry at your school? How did you get through it?

_____

_____

_____

What will you do in the future when you struggle with campus ministry?_____

_____

_____

Don't forget that you are not called to reach your school alone. Yes, the Holy Spirit is with you, but so are other students.

Come together as a team to see God overflow at your school!

W2 OVERFLOW
MONDAY
DATE:_____

☐ Read: Acts 8 ☐ 30min Personal Prayer ☐ 15min Worship
☐ DAILY CHALLENGE:

Today, go out of your way to show LOVE to someone
who is not in your normal social group.

What did God say to you in personal prayer time?
_____

_____

What scripture stood out to you from the daily reading?
_____

_____

What did this scripture reveal to you? _____

_____

_____

How does this understanding apply to your life? _____

_____

_____

We encourage you to write down a prayer that God would help
you live out this understanding. _____

_____

_____

P24

My appointment with
God tomorrow is at _____:_____

W2 OVERFLOW

TUESDAY   **DATE:**_____

☐ Read: Acts 9 ☐ 30min Personal Prayer ☐ 15min Worship
☐ DAILY CHALLENGE:

Today, commit to always walk in JOY.
Even when situations do not go your way, remember...
"The joy of the Lord is my strength." Neh. 8:10

What did God say to you in personal prayer time?

_____

_____

What scripture stood out to you from the daily reading?

_____

_____

What did this scripture reveal to you? _____

_____

_____

How does this understanding apply to your life? _____

_____

_____

We encourage you to write down a prayer that God would help
you live out this understanding. _____

_____

_____

My appointment with
God tomorrow is at   _____ : _____

W2 OVERFLOW
WEDNESDAY
DATE:_____

☐ Read: Acts10 ☐ 30min Personal Prayer ☐ 15min Worship
☐ DAILY CHALLENGE:

Today, show FAITHFULNESS to your youth pastor by
arriving early to help set up for the service.

What did God say to you in personal prayer time?

_____

_____

What scripture stood out to you from the daily reading?

_____

_____

What did this scripture reveal to you? _____

_____

_____

How does this understanding apply to your life? _____

_____

_____

We encourage you to write down a prayer that God would help
you live out this understanding. _____

_____

_____

My appointment with
God tomorrow is at   _____:_____

W2 OVERFLOW

THURSDAY **DATE:**_____

☐ Read: Acts 11 ☐ 30min Personal Prayer ☐ 15min Worship
☐ DAILY CHALLENGE:

Go to the Youth Alive App and watch a podcast under
the resources "Grow" tab!

What did God say to you in personal prayer time?

_____

_____

What scripture stood out to you from the daily reading?

_____

_____

What did this scripture reveal to you? _____

_____

_____

How does this understanding apply to your life? _____

_____

_____

We encourage you to write down a prayer that God would help
you live out this understanding. _____

_____

_____

My appointment with
God tomorrow is at _____ : _____

P27

W2 OVERFLOW
FRIDAY

DATE:_____

☐ Read: Acts12 ☐ 30min Personal Prayer ☐ 15min Worship
☐ DAILY CHALLENGE:

Today, strive to make PEACE with anyone that you don't like
or who doesn't like you.

What did God say to you in personal prayer time?

_____

_____

What scripture stood out to you from the daily reading?

_____

_____

What did this scripture reveal to you? _____

_____

_____

How does this understanding apply to your life? _____

_____

_____

We encourage you to write down a prayer that God would help
you live out this understanding. _____

_____

_____

My appointment with
God tomorrow is at _____ : _____

W2 OVERFLOW

SATURDAY   **DATE:**_____

☐ Read: Acts13 ☐ 30min Personal Prayer ☐ 15min Worship
☐ DAILY CHALLENGE:

Today, commit to choose GENTLENESS by having the
right attitude in every situation.

What did God say to you in personal prayer time?

_____

_____

What scripture stood out to you from the daily reading?

_____

_____

What did this scripture reveal to you? _____

_____

_____

How does this understanding apply to your life? _____

_____

_____

We encourage you to write down a prayer that God would help
you live out this understanding. _____

_____

_____

My appointment with
God tomorrow is at   _____ : _____

P29

W2 OVERFLOW
SUNDAY

DATE:_____

☐ Read: Acts14 ☐ 30min Personal Prayer ☐ 15min Worship
☐ DAILY CHALLENGE:

Today, strive to have more SELF-CONTROL by not criticizing, tearing down, or being negatively sarcastic to anyone.

What did God say to you in personal prayer time?

_____

_____

What scripture stood out to you from the daily reading?

_____

_____

What did this scripture reveal to you? _____

_____

_____

How does this understanding apply to your life? _____

_____

_____

We encourage you to write down a prayer that God would help you live out this understanding. _____

_____

_____

P30

My appointment with
God tomorrow is at   _____ : _____

W2 OVERFLOW

NOTES :

_____

_____

_____

_____

_____

_____

_____

PRAYER LIST :

Revival	Your Church	Your School
Family	Your Pastors	Your Principal
Friends	Missions	Your Teachers
The Lost	Personal Growth	Administration

_____

_____

_____

_____

_____

_____

W3 EMPOWERED TO WITNESS

The top reasons students do not share the Gospel:
- "I don't know how to start the conversation."
- "Honestly, it's just not that important to me."
- "I'm afraid of being rejected or looking stupid."

Every person struggles with some kind of fear or insecurity. Can you identify yours? _____

Every fear and insecurity has a root. Perhaps yours is from your past, a traumatic experience, or a person who made you feel rejected. Where do you think your fear comes from? _____

What is your biggest fear when it comes to sharing the Gospel?

_____

Fear is debilitating, destroying, and defeating. That is exactly why the Apostle Paul tells Timothy:

"Therefore I remind you to stir up the gift of God, which is in you by the laying on of my hands. For God has not given us the spirit of fear, but of power, and love, and self-control."   **2 Timothy 1:6-7 (MEV)**

→ This verse reminds us that fear is not from God. Rather, His Holy Spirit fills us with POWER, LOVE, and a SOUND MIND.

→ The beginning of this verse also tells us to STIR UP THE GIFT OF GOD. Why? Look at the next line, "Because God has not given us a Spirit of fear."

Using our GIFTS is directly related to overcoming FEAR!

→ What areas has God gifted you in? Painting, music, speaking, organization, hospitality, or maybe graphics?

If you are afraid to witness, start by using the gifts that God given you at your campus... Then, you will grow more bold!

P32

Student Story...

Garrett was a junior in high school when he realized that God was calling him to be a worship pastor. After his dad and step-dad both walked out, Garrett struggled with pain and fear, but he did not allow it to hold him back. So, he grabbed his guitar, some friends, and started leading worship at his school during a campus club. Garrett also began inviting his unsaved friends. Before he knew it, the club began to grow. Many people came to know Jesus because Garret stepped out in courage. Today, he travels the nation as a signed musician and worship leader, but it all started when he chose to use his gift to reach his school.

Garrett became a witness, or someone who testifies about Jesus Christ in words and actions. Do you want to break free from fear and become a bold witness? Ask the Holy Spirit to fill you with power. Then, start using your gifts like Garrett did!

What talents or gifts do you have that you can use for God at your campus? _____

_____

We are filled with POWER when the Holy Spirit comes on us so that we can be a WITNESS to all people in all places! (Read Acts 1:8 NLT)

Remember, we are a witness when we use our gifts AND when we have conversations with others about Jesus. Sometimes it is easier to use our gifts than it is to start conversations, but we must do both.

Here are some ideas to help you witness through conversations:
Use Your Testimony: Know your story and use it. Go share the Gospel using the stories of what God has done in your life.

Memorize Scripture: Romans 1:16, Romans 3:23, and John 10:10 are powerful scriptures for witnessing conversations. Memorize as many as you can.

Other Conversation Starters: Ask if they need prayer; Try to do something nice for them without expecting anything in return; Give a word of encouragement.

P33

WHAT DOES THIS MEAN FOR MY CAMPUS?

Filled with the Holy Spirit, Taylor knew she was called to witness to a girl at school named Summer. But Summer wanted nothing to do with God. At first, Taylor would invite Summer to church or ask if she needed prayer. Each effort was met with resistance. This did not stop Taylor. Day after day she continued to love Summer and be a witness. After months of praying, Summer finally went to church with Taylor where she surrendered her life to God.

Your efforts may be met with a negative response, but this DOES NOT mean you failed. The win is that you obeyed God—the rest is up to the Holy Spirit. Learn to shake off rejection, because you never know God's ultimate plan. Just ask Summer and Taylor, who are now best friends. They attend church together and lead a campus movement at their high school.

THINK ABOUT IT...

How can you use your gifts to be a witness at your school?

_____

_____

Write the three people God is putting on your heart to witness to.

_____

How can you start conversations with these people about Jesus?

_____

_____

_____

The righteous are as BOLD as a LION (Prov 28:1).
Don't let the enemy silence you; deal with your fear TODAY.
The Holy Spirit empowers you to ROAR, so lets be as bold as a lion.

WITNESS REPORT

Sometimes the best way to witness is by sharing one of your stories. You wrote out your testimony already, so consider using it to share about Jesus. Then, record your experience here.

_____

_____

_____

_____

_____

_____

_____

_____

_____

_____

_____

_____

_____

_____

_____

_____

W3 WITNESS
MONDAY

DATE:_____

☐ Read: Acts15 ☐ 30min Personal Prayer ☐ 15min Worship
☐ DAILY CHALLENGE:

Pray and ask the Holy Spirit to fill you to be a better witness. If you are filled, then pray in the Spirit and ask Jesus to fill you fresh. Take this seriously—this is how empowerment happens.

What did God say to you in personal prayer time?

_____

_____

What scripture stood out to you from the daily reading?

_____

_____

What did this scripture reveal to you? _____

_____

_____

How does this understanding apply to your life? _____

_____

_____

We encourage you to write down a prayer that God would help you live out this understanding. _____

_____

_____

My appointment with
God tomorrow is at   _____:_____

W3 WITNESS

☐ Read: Acts16 ☐ 30min Personal Prayer ☐ 15min Worship
☐ DAILY CHALLENGE:

Plan to witness to at least one person this week. Then, share
about your experience on the witness report page,
found on Page 35.

What did God say to you in personal prayer time?

_____

_____

What scripture stood out to you from the daily reading?

_____

_____

What did this scripture reveal to you? _____

_____

_____

How does this understanding apply to your life? _____

_____

_____

We encourage you to write down a prayer that God would help
you live out this understanding. _____

_____

_____

W3 WITNESS

WEDNESDAY

DATE:_____

☐ Read: Acts17 ☐ 30min Personal Prayer ☐ 15min Worship
☐ DAILY CHALLENGE:

Pray for three friends that need Jesus. Ask God to open a door for you to be able to witness to one of them this week.

What did God say to you in personal prayer time?

_____

_____

What scripture stood out to you from the daily reading?

_____

_____

What did this scripture reveal to you? _____

_____

_____

How does this understanding apply to your life? _____

_____

_____

We encourage you to write down a prayer that God would help you live out this understanding. _____

_____

_____

P38

My appointment with
God tomorrow is at _____ : _____

W3 WITNESS

THURSDAY   **DATE:**_____

☐ Read: Acts18 ☐ 30min Personal Prayer ☐ 15min Worship
☐ DAILY CHALLENGE:

Today, deal with any fears you may have about witnessing. Pray
about it, talk to someone, or find a Scripture to help you.

What did God say to you in personal prayer time?

_____

_____

What scripture stood out to you from the daily reading?

_____

_____

What did this scripture reveal to you? _____

_____

_____

How does this understanding apply to your life? _____

_____

_____

We encourage you to write down a prayer that God would help
you live out this understanding. _____

_____

_____

My appointment with
God tomorrow is at   _____ : _____

P39

W3 WITNESS

FRIDAY   **DATE:**_____

☐ Read: Acts19 ☐ 30min Personal Prayer ☐ 15min Worship
☐ DAILY CHALLENGE:

Memorize at least one of the three Scriptures from this week's lesson that will help you in witnessing conversations.

What did God say to you in personal prayer time?

_____

_____

What scripture stood out to you from the daily reading?

_____

_____

What did this scripture reveal to you? _____

_____

_____

How does this understanding apply to your life? _____

_____

_____

We encourage you to write down a prayer that God would help you live out this understanding. _____

_____

_____

My appointment with God tomorrow is at _____ : _____

W3 WITNESS

SATURDAY   **DATE:**_____

☐ Read: Acts20 ☐ 30min Personal Prayer ☐ 15min Worship
☐ DAILY CHALLENGE:

Pray that God would show you how to use your gifts to be a
witness at school and help you start conversations
about Jesus. Both of these are important!

What did God say to you in personal prayer time?

_____

_____

What scripture stood out to you from the daily reading?

_____

_____

What did this scripture reveal to you? _____

_____

_____

How does this understanding apply to your life? _____

_____

_____

We encourage you to write down a prayer that God would help
you live out this understanding. _____

_____

_____

My appointment with
God tomorrow is at   _____ : _____

P41

W3 WITNESS
SUNDAY   DATE:_____

☐ Read: Acts21 ☐ 30min Personal Prayer ☐ 15min Worship
☐ DAILY CHALLENGE:

This week you were asked to witness to at least one person about Jesus. Today, make sure you have done this and filled out the witness report. Consider sharing your experience with someone.

What did God say to you in personal prayer time?

_____

_____

What scripture stood out to you from the daily reading?

_____

_____

What did this scripture reveal to you? _____

_____

_____

How does this understanding apply to your life? _____

_____

_____

We encourage you to write down a prayer that God would help you live out this understanding. _____

_____

_____

My appointment with
God tomorrow is at _____ : _____

W3 WITNESS

NOTES :

_____

_____

_____

_____

_____

_____

_____

_____

PRAYER LIST :

Revival	Your Church	Your School
Family	Your Pastors	Your Principal
Friends	Missions	Your Teachers
The Lost	Personal Growth	Administration

_____

_____

_____

_____

_____

_____

_____

W4 EMPOWERD TO EVANGELIZE

To evangelize is to do the work of an evangelist. This means,

LET YOUR LIFE PREACH THE GOSPEL

YOU are the best **EVANGELIST** that will
EVER walk onto your campus!

How?

1. LIVE AS A SERVANT-LEADER

We must lead like Jesus by serving others. Your age is no indication of your ability to lead. If you are a Christian, you are already leading.

As a SERVANT LEADER, your mouth is one of the first indicators of your Christianity →

- **Build up others** (Ephesians 4:29)

- **Watch your words** - the tongue holds the power of life or death. (Proverbs 18:21)

- **Watch your joking** - if it doesn't build up others it shouldn't be said. (Ephesians 5:4)

As a SERVANT LEADER, you have an opportunity to start a Campus Movement →

Every school needs a campus movement—this may be a club, prayer time, Bible study, or missions movement. Every campus movement needs a leader. Why couldn't this be you? If there is a campus movement already at your school, we encourage you to get involved. Otherwise, pray about starting one yourself. For more info, check out the ideas on the Youth Alive App and talk to your youth pastor!

2. BE LED IN LOVE BY THE SPIRIT

Look at what one youth pastor does with her students:
"We play ultimate frisbee and pray on the middle school campus. One of the students in our youth group reached out to a group of kids that went there, which led them to come to our youth service, get saved, and then get baptized!" Pastor Vienna Pearl - Key West, FL

Let the Spirit lead you to the people, places, and moments that He wants to use you in. Being led in love means looking for a chance to serve. What can you do to serve your school in a fresh way?

3. LOOK PAST YOUR GROUP

Did you know that 47% of students say that their social life would end if they did not have a phone? [1]

Wow! Do not fall into the trap of thinking that your world is made up of your direct family and friends. There is a world beyond your fingertips!

In high school, it seems like the smallest issues can sometimes be the end of the world. But in order to evangelize, we must get outside of our small world of technology and drama in order to THINK BIGGER.

→ **Looking past your group also means** understanding that every person in your school—regardless of background, age, or social status—deserves to hear about Jesus. This is the greatest "human right" that will ever exist in our world. We **SERVE** so that when the opportunity arises we can **SHARE** about Jesus! Brainstorm about ways to reach others outside of your normal circle of friends.

Do you want to know more about The Human Right Movement? *www.thehumanright.org*

→ **Looking past your group also means** giving, so that missionaries can **GO** share about Jesus in other countries. This can be done by raising money for Speed the Light.

WHAT DOES THIS MEAN FOR MY CAMPUS?

THINK ABOUT IT...

How did the disciples continue to evangelize after Jesus left earth?

_____

_____

_____

How can you "Let your Life Preach the Gospel?"

_____

_____

_____

Did you know that 82% of people say that they would come to church if they were simply asked? [2]

When is the last time you invited someone from school to your youth ministry? _____

Can people at your school tell that you are a Christian, based on the life that you live? _____

If not, there is still time to change!

"And I pray that the sharing of your faith may become effective for the full knowledge of every good thing that is in us for the sake of Christ." Philemon 1:6 (ESV)

P46

"Teenagers are not the future, they are the present. They are the now! In John 10:10 we are told that Christ came to give us abundant life. God is using teenagers now to bring abundance to their campuses; to overflow with joy, hope, freedom and love. As teenagers boldly walk in the abundance of Christ, their households, classrooms, and campuses will start to change.

Pastor Ashely Hudson - Ocala, FL

P47

W4 EVANGELIZE

MONDAY   **DATE:**_____

☐ Read: Acts22 ☐ 30min Personal Prayer ☐ 15min Worship
☐ DAILY CHALLENGE:

Post your favorite Bible verse on social media and tag
@pfyouthalive so that we can see it.

What did God say to you in personal prayer time?

_____

_____

What scripture stood out to you from the daily reading?

_____

_____

What did this scripture reveal to you? _____

_____

_____

How does this understanding apply to your life? _____

_____

_____

We encourage you to write down a prayer that God would help
you live out this understanding. _____

_____

_____

My appointment with
                    God tomorrow is at   _____ : _____

W4 EVANGELIZE

TUESDAY   **DATE:**_____

☐ Read: Acts23 ☐ 30min Personal Prayer ☐ 15min Worship
☐ DAILY CHALLENGE:

Today, buy someone at school a soda or a snack, just because
you want to bless them.

What did God say to you in personal prayer time?

_____

_____

What scripture stood out to you from the daily reading?

_____

_____

What did this scripture reveal to you? _____

_____

_____

How does this understanding apply to your life? _____

_____

_____

We encourage you to write down a prayer that God would help
you live out this understanding. _____

_____

_____

My appointment with
God tomorrow is at   _____ : _____

P49

W4 EVANGELIZE

WEDNESDAY   **DATE:**_____

☐ Read: Acts24 ☐ 30min Personal Prayer ☐ 15min Worship
☐ DAILY CHALLENGE:

Write a letter of encouragement for someone and give it to them.

What did God say to you in personal prayer time?

_____

_____

What scripture stood out to you from the daily reading?

_____

_____

What did this scripture reveal to you? _____

_____

_____

How does this understanding apply to your life? _____

_____

_____

We encourage you to write down a prayer that God would help
you live out this understanding. _____

_____

_____

P50

My appointment with
God tomorrow is at   _____ : _____

W4 EVANGELIZE

THURSDAY   **DATE:**_____

☐ Read: Acts25 ☐ 30min Personal Prayer ☐ 15min Worship
☐ DAILY CHALLENGE:

Today, find someone outside your normal group
and encourage them.

What did God say to you in personal prayer time?

_____

_____

What scripture stood out to you from the daily reading?

_____

_____

What did this scripture reveal to you? _____

_____

_____

How does this understanding apply to your life? _____

_____

_____

We encourage you to write down a prayer that God would help
you live out this understanding. _____

_____

_____

My appointment with
God tomorrow is at   _____ : _____

P51

W4 EVANGELIZE

FRIDAY   **DATE:**_____

☐ Read: Acts26 ☐ 30min Personal Prayer ☐ 15min Worship
☐ DAILY CHALLENGE:

Invite someone to go to church with you next week.
Then, actually follow through and bring them!

What did God say to you in personal prayer time?

_____

_____

What scripture stood out to you from the daily reading?

_____

_____

What did this scripture reveal to you? _____

_____

_____

How does this understanding apply to your life? _____

_____

_____

We encourage you to write down a prayer that God would help
you live out this understanding. _____

_____

_____

P52   My appointment with
               God tomorrow is at   _____ : _____

W4 EVANGELIZE
SATURDAY   DATE:_____

☐ Read: Acts27 ☐ 30min Personal Prayer ☐ 15min Worship
☐ DAILY CHALLENGE:

Today, ask someone if you can pray with them for a
struggle or obstacle they may be going through.

What did God say to you in personal prayer time?

_____

_____

What scripture stood out to you from the daily reading?

_____

_____

What did this scripture reveal to you? _____

_____

_____

How does this understanding apply to your life? _____

_____

_____

We encourage you to write down a prayer that God would help
you live out this understanding. _____

_____

_____

My appointment with
God tomorrow is at   _____ : _____

P53

W4 EVANGELIZE

SUNDAY   **DATE:**_____

☐ Read: Acts28 ☐ 30min Personal Prayer ☐ 15min Worship
☐ DAILY CHALLENGE:

Go to the Youth Alive App and watch a podcast on outreach.

What did God say to you in personal prayer time?

_____

_____

What scripture stood out to you from the daily reading?

_____

_____

What did this scripture reveal to you? _____

_____

_____

How does this understanding apply to your life? _____

_____

_____

We encourage you to write down a prayer that God would help
you live out this understanding. _____

_____

_____

P54   My appointment with
God tomorrow is at   _____ : _____

W4 EVANGELIZE

NOTES :

_____

_____

_____

_____

_____

_____

_____

_____

PRAYER LIST :

Revival	Your Church	Your School
Family	Your Pastors	Your Principal
Friends	Missions	Your Teachers
The Lost	Personal Growth	Administration

_____

_____

_____

_____

_____

_____

W5 EMPOWERED TO RECEIVE

Over Christmas break of 1900, a Bible professor sent his students home to research the Holy Spirit. Each student came back with the same finding: every time a disciple was baptized with the Holy Spirit they spoke in other tongues. This class decided to put their theory into action, so Professor Parham called a prayer service on 12/31/1900. During the service, one student felt called to be a missionary. That night, the professor remembers praying for this student: **"I had scarcely repeated three dozen sentences when a glory fell upon her, a halo seemed to surround her head and face, and she began speaking in the Chinese language, and was unable to speak English for three days. When she tried to write in English... she wrote in Chinese, copies of which we still have in newspapers printed at that time."**

The prayer meeting continued for days, with many people receiving the Holy Spirit, but it didn't stop there. Revival spread to Azusa Street in California, and from the Azusa Street Revival, many of the denominations we know of today were birthed! [1]

Where did it all start?
Students. In a prayer service. 100+ years ago.

You are EMPOWERED TO RECEIVE.

"You will receive power when the Holy Spirit comes on you and you will be my witnesses..." Acts 1:8

This is the chain-breaking, devil-fleeing, miracle-working power of God that is alive in every believer. The same power that raised Jesus from the dead dwells inside of you! We do not SEEK the power and it is NOT about a denomination. Instead, we seek JESUS and the POWER will flow!

Everyone responds differently to the Spirit's power. David danced, Moses shook, and Daniel fell down like he was dead. The lame man jumped and on the Day of Pentecost, 120 of the disciples received the gift of speaking in other languages.

P56

This gift is not just for the disciples! Let's take a closer look at the gift of speaking in other tongues:

WHAT IS TONGUES	It's a language for intimacy.(1Corinthians 14:2) And a language for war (Ephesians 6:10-18)
WHY TONGUES?	The tongue is set on fire from hell; only the Holy Spirit can tame the tongue! (James 3:6-8)
WHO?	Everyone! (1Corinthians 14:5)
WHEN DO YOU PRAY IN TONGUES?	"Friend, don't let the enemy dupe you into thinking you shouldn't pray in tongues. Cast down his thoughts and push past those feelings. Open your mouth daily and carefully build yourselves up in this most holy faith by praying in the Holy Spirit." (Jude 1:20 MSG)

→ Receiving the gift of tongues ←

In the same way that you receive salvation by faith, you receive the gift of the Holy Spirit! Ask with a heart full of faith and you will receive (Mt. 21:22)! It may not be in the time or place you expect, but God is faithful. Don't be afraid to ask and don't be afraid when the power of the Holy Spirit fills you. Remember, God loves you and wants you to receive all that he has for you. Pray and wait, because God will not disappoint!

→ Other Gift's of the Holy Spirit ←

The Spirit also empowered the disciples by giving them spiritual gifts. In the same way, the Holy Spirit also gives you the Gifts of the Spirit, so that you can do what God calls you to do!

Here are some of the gifts: (1Corinthians 12:8-10)

Wisdom	Healing	Discerning of Spirits
Knowledge	Miracles	Speaking in Tongues
Faith	Prophecy	Interpretation of Tongues

WHAT DOES THIS MEAN FOR MY CAMPUS?

GOD'S NOT DONE YET!

Two gangs put down their weapons and, with 400 other students, gathered to hear an assembly message presented at Roosevelt High School. On that day, the Holy Spirit came into the room and students began to weep. A teacher who had grown up as an evangelist's kid stated that he had never seen an outpouring of the Holy Spirit the way he did that day at this public high school.

The revival continued! Even to this day the teacher explains, *"Many days you see kids with tears asking Christ to come into their hearts."* God is continuing the work he began on this campus two years ago! [2]

Do you believe this could happen at your school?
It is in the darkest places that God's light shines the brightest. Don't give up on your school—Gods not done yet!

GET READY FOR AN OUTPOURING!

Continually pray for the Holy Spirit to fill you, but don't be surprised when he lets you feel his power through giving you spiritual gifts and allowing you to experience his presence.

After you are filled with the gift of speaking in tongues, we encourage you to daily build yourself up by speaking in tongues. Make this a regular part of your prayers and watch God pour out of your life! This will give you boldness to be a witness in your world!

GIFTS OF THE SPIRIT - WHICH ONES DO I HAVE?

We are also told to be led in love AND EARNESTLY seek after ALL the gifts of the spirit!! (1Corinthians 14:1) **To help you with this, take the Spiritual Gifts Assessment found on the Youth Alive App under resources.** The purpose is to help you at serving the Lord on your campus and youth ministry.

P58

THINK ABOUT IT...

After taking the assessment, what are your top three spiritual gifts?

_____

_____

How can you use these gifts to impact your campus in a greater way?

_____

_____

Here are two students who used their gifts to change their world:

"Sarah loved praying for people and felt like she had the gift of faith. So, she started praying for people at school. The sport teams began sending hurting people to her so that she would pray for them. Her reputation spread as the girl who prays for people, and they get better."

"Kent started using his gift of administration to help his school office file papers. This opened a door for him to invite the Youth Alive team to his school to do an assembly program. The administration even allowed him to pray at his graduation."

These are just a few ideas! But don't forget....It's All About LOVE.

We cannot get so caught up in our gifts that we forget to serve God outside of our comfort zone. Just because we have a gift to teach, it does not mean that we should avoid stacking chairs. **Love must be the rule that guides our actions.**

W5 RECEIVE

MONDAY   **DATE:**_____

☐ Read: Luke24 ☐ 30min Personal Prayer ☐ 15min Worship
☐ DAILY CHALLENGE:

Take the spiritual gifts assessment on the Youth Alive App. This will show you the spiritual gifts that God is developing in your life!

What did God say to you in personal prayer time?

_____

_____

What scripture stood out to you from the daily reading?

_____

_____

What did this scripture reveal to you? _____

_____

_____

How does this understanding apply to your life? _____

_____

_____

We encourage you to write down a prayer that God would help you live out this understanding. _____

_____

_____

My appointment with God tomorrow is at _____ : _____

W5 RECEIVE

TUESDAY   **DATE:**_____

☐ Read: 1Cor.12   ☐ 30min Personal Prayer   ☐ 15min Worship
☐ DAILY CHALLENGE:

In your prayer time, ask the Holy Spirit to show you how you can use your spiritual gifts at school. Talk to your youth pastor, small group, or campus group about these ideas.

What did God say to you in personal prayer time?

_____

_____

What scripture stood out to you from the daily reading?

_____

_____

What did this scripture reveal to you? _____

_____

_____

How does this understanding apply to your life? _____

_____

_____

We encourage you to write down a prayer that God would help you live out this understanding. _____

_____

_____

My appointment with God tomorrow is at   _____ : _____

P61

W5 RECEIVE

WEDNESDAY   DATE:_____

☐ Read: Matt. 3 ☐ 30min Personal Prayer ☐ 15min Worship
☐ DAILY CHALLENGE:

Go to the concordance in your Bible and find a few Scriptures on the Holy Spirit. Write them down and regularly pray for the Holy Spirit to pour out at your school.

What did God say to you in personal prayer time?

_____

_____

What scripture stood out to you from the daily reading?

_____

_____

What did this scripture reveal to you? _____

_____

_____

How does this understanding apply to your life? _____

_____

_____

We encourage you to write down a prayer that God would help you live out this understanding. _____

_____

_____

My appointment with
                God tomorrow is at   _____:_____

W5 RECEIVE

THURSDAY   DATE:_____

☐ Read: Romans 8 ☐ 30min Personal Prayer ☐ 15min Worship
☐ DAILY CHALLENGE:

Go to the Youth Alive App and read one of the Blogs!

What did God say to you in personal prayer time?

_____

_____

What scripture stood out to you from the daily reading?

_____

_____

What did this scripture reveal to you? _____

_____

_____

How does this understanding apply to your life? _____

_____

_____

We encourage you to write down a prayer that God would help
you live out this understanding. _____

_____

_____

My appointment with
God tomorrow is at   _____ : _____

P63

W5 RECEIVE

DATE:_____

☐ Read: 1John 4 ☐30min Personal Prayer ☐15min Worship
☐ DAILY CHALLENGE:

Today, allot half of your designated prayer time to praying in
tongues. If you are not filled with this gift, then we challenge you
to focus on growing closer to Jesus in this area.

What did God say to you in personal prayer time?

_____

_____

What scripture stood out to you from the daily reading?

_____

_____

What did this scripture reveal to you? _____

_____

_____

How does this understanding apply to your life? _____

_____

_____

We encourage you to write down a prayer that God would help
you live out this understanding. _____

_____

_____

My appointment with
God tomorrow is at   _____ : _____

W5 RECEIVE

SATURDAY   **DATE:**_____

☐ Read: John 14 ☐ 30min Personal Prayer ☐ 15min Worship
☐ DAILY CHALLENGE:

Today, spend some extra time praying for revival
to spark at your school!

What did God say to you in personal prayer time?

_____

_____

What scripture stood out to you from the daily reading?

_____

_____

What did this scripture reveal to you? _____

_____

_____

How does this understanding apply to your life? _____

_____

_____

We encourage you to write down a prayer that God would help
you live out this understanding. _____

_____

_____

My appointment with
God tomorrow is at   _____ : _____

P65

W5 RECEIVE

SUNDAY   **DATE:**_____

☐ Read: Joel 2   ☐ 30min Personal Prayer   ☐ 15min Worship
☐ DAILY CHALLENGE:

Find a group of people to commit to pray with you on a weekly basis for revival in your school. This may look different at each campus, so do not grow discouraged!

What did God say to you in personal prayer time?

_____

_____

What scripture stood out to you from the daily reading?

_____

_____

What did this scripture reveal to you? _____

_____

_____

How does this understanding apply to your life? _____

_____

_____

We encourage you to write down a prayer that God would help you live out this understanding. _____

_____

_____

P66   **My appointment with God tomorrow is at** _____ : _____

W5 RECEIVE

NOTES :

_____

_____

_____

_____

_____

_____

_____

_____

PRAYER LIST :

Revival	Your Church	Your School
Family	Your Pastors	Your Principal
Friends	Missions	Your Teachers
The Lost	Personal Growth	Administration

_____

_____

_____

_____

_____

_____

MY MISSIONARY STORY

Congratulations, you finished the EmpowerME Challenge. Show us your completed book at the next PFYouth event and you will get a free Youth Alive T-shirt.

But, there is still one more story to write. In fact, it is the most important story in this journey... Your Story.

Describe what you have learned about God and yourself over the last five weeks: _____

_____

_____

_____

_____

_____

_____

What have you done over the past five weeks that you never thought you would be able to do: _____

_____

_____

_____

_____

_____

What are you going to do to keep your time with God a priority:

_____

_____

What is something that happened in the past five weeks that blew your mind?_____

_____

_____

_____

What is your God dream for your campus this year?_____

_____

_____

_____

_____

_____

_____

This is your final part of this journey, but the truth is that this story never ends. Continue writing your own missionary stories!

FINAL PRAYER...

The power of the Holy Spirit is meant for TODAY, as long as you choose to RECEIVE all that God has for you!

We cannot continue to do campus ministry without acknowledging the Holy Spirit as the one who fills us with power. Do you want to be an effective Campus Missionary? You need more of the Holy Spirit!

Today, God wants to fill you with power.
Pray this prayer from your heart →

"Holy Spirit, Thank you for taking me deeper during the EmpowerME Challenge. I receive all of the gifts that you have for me and I seal all the work that you did in my life. Thank you for filling me with power as I surrender to Jesus. Please continue to fill me fresh and empower me to speak in the heavenly language that you have for me. Thank you for being my friend, comforter, and guide." AMEN.

It is time to live a life of POWER!

P - Prayer
O - Overflow
W - Witness
E - Evangelize
R - Receive

P70

THE CHALLENGE CONTINUES

YOU MADE IT THROUGH THE EMPOWERME CHALLENGE!

We know it's not easy reaching your school, but God never said it would be easy—only that it would be worth it. If you continue surrendering to God and walking in the power of the Holy Spirit, the possibility for miracles at your campus are endless!

So, don't forget...
YOU ARE NOT ALONE.
The Holy Spirit is always with you.
YOU CAN DO THIS.
The Holy Spirit empowers you.
AND WE BELIEVE IN YOU.

The secret is that the EmpowerME challenge should never stop. You should always be reading your Bible, praying, worshiping, and challenging yourself to reach your friends.

SO, GO CHANGE YOUR WORLD! WE ARE PROUD OF YOU!

Joe and Natalie Barnoske
@joebarnoske | @nataliebarnoske | @pfyouthalive
Email: barnoske@yapfl.com
Web: pfyouthalive.com

We would love to hear what God did in your life during this challenge. Contact us at any of our social media accounts and we can talk!

P71

CAMPUS MISSIONARY COMMITMENTS

If you are not a campus missionary, please download the PF Youth Alive App and sign up! This will keep you connected to the campus missionary community.

A CAMPUS MISSIONARY IS A STUDENT WHO COMMITS TO BE A LEADER ON GOD'S MISSION TO THEIR SCHOOL.

→ **These are the five core commitments of a campus missionary**

PRAY at all times
LIVE like Jesus
TELL the world
SERVE your school
GIVE to missions

I _____commit to follow the five campus missionary commitments. With the help of the Holy Spirit, I promise to try to be the best leader that I can be.

Signature:

_____

You can tear this page out and keep it
where you can regularly see it!

P72

ABOUT PF YOUTH ALIVE

Youth Alive is a ministry of PF Youth that seeks to equip and empower the next generation to reach every student in every school across Florida. By raising up students to be Campus Missionaries, initiating campus movements, and facilitating cutting edge school assemblies, PF Youth Alive is the premier resource for campus ministry.

The PF Youth Alive App is the central hub of all of our resources. You will find a new podcast and blog every month of the school year. You will also find videos, lessons, campus club resources, and much more!

Want to make a donation or help support PF Youth Alive? PFYouthAlive.com is the main resource for leader and partner information.

ABOUT THE AUTHORS

There are approximately 1,500,000 middle and high school students in the state of Florida. In fact, the schools constitute one of the largest mission fields in all of America. Every day young people are faced with a choice to live for God or fall into the temptations of their generation.

This burden led Natalie and Joe Barnoske to become Youth Alive Missionaries.

Natalie and Joe Barnoske are gifted communicators who carry a passion to see a generation of students arise in boldness and spark revival. They have both served as youth pastors and evangelists individually, and now serve as Youth Alive missionaries together in Florida. Natalie and Joe both hold bachelors degree's in ministry from Warner University and are ordained with the Assemblies of God. They love staying active, especially with Samson, their chihuahua.

To learn more about their ministry, visit www.pfyouthalive.com.

NOTES

LESSON 1

1. Statistics taken from Gallup Pole Finds, Pastor's Weekly Briefing 12/24/04, and Foster Letter 6/04

2. Tim Tedow quote - http://www.brainyquote.com/quotes/quotes/t/timtebow440887.html

3. Tim Tebow quote - http://www.brainyquote.com/quotes/quotes/t/timtebow550705.html

LESSON 2

1. Tim Tebow quote - http://www.brainyquote.com/quotes/quotes/t/timtebow550708.html

LESSON 4

1. Statistics taken from CTIA and Harris Interactive http://www.harrisinteractive.com/NewsRoom/PressReleases/tabid/446/ctl/ReadCustom%20Default/mid/1506/ArticleId/191/Default.aspx

2. Thom S. Rainer, The Unchurched Next Door:Understanding Faith Stages as Keys to Sharing Your Faith (Grand Rapids: Zondervan, 2003)

LESSON 5

1. Assemblies of God Beginning - http://www.revival-library.org/pensketches/am_pentecostals/parham.htmlSchool

2. Revival - http://blog.godreports.com/2015/01/extraordinary-revival-in-l-a-and-orange-county-high-schools/

Made in the USA
San Bernardino, CA
28 September 2015